THE SECRET OF MANIFESTING YOUR LOVE

USING THE LAW OF ATTRACTION TO ATTRACT A PARTICULAR PERSON

By

Lydia S. Rodriguez

Content

Chapter 1

Introduction

This comprehensive manual offers the key to successfully attracting love and manifesting a certain individual.
Write your love tale now and begin living it!
Okay, so you want to manifest a particular individual. You have your sights set on a particular person who you can't stop thinking about. You're crushing it!
Your heart races when you think of this person. And you are very certain

that you intended to be with them. Nobody else will do it because your mind is completely made up.

That's who it MUST be.

Then this manual is your golden ticket to a happily ever after with the prince or princess of your choice, my love-struck friend.

So fasten your seatbelt and prepare. Because the person you've been pining for is going to fall head over heels in love with you six ways to Sunday!

Consider me to be your fairy godmother as I teach you how to use the Law of Attraction to bring love into your life.

And more precisely, how to make love come true with your particular partner.

Before we begin using our magic wand to turn your desires into reality, let's

address the query that initially drew you to this page.

Is it possible to genuinely fall in love with someone?

Your ex, a crush, a buddy you want to fall in love with, or even someone who has no idea you even exist?

YES! A certain person is possible to manifest!

Let me start by stating that it is certainly, positively possible to create the person you desire. Since EVERYTHING IS POSSIBLE. PERIOD.

Anything is simple to manifest. It's a gift that God gave us naturally, and we use it constantly. every day and every second.
I won't lie to you, though.

Before you can successfully materialize what you desire, you might need to put in some effort if your subconscious harbors a lot of self-defeating thoughts or if you have trouble maintaining high-vibrational emotions.
You'll have to make a daily commitment to forming new behaviors.
However, you'll be able to manifest right away once you raise your vibration, get rid of old limiting ideas,

and adhere to the instructions in this article.

There are no coincidences in our universe.

A set of laws govern how the cosmos functions. laws that everyone must abide by selecting your sensibility and what you bring into it becomes an exceptionally practical idea once you have a good understanding of how those principles operate.

Because there are no coincidences in the universe. Therefore, attracting a particular individual into your life is not woo-woo.

It all makes sense when you consider how reality functions.

Just before, we had no idea how to play the game. How to benefit from these universal laws. Nobody ever took us aside and handed us a manual of rules.

Till now...

It has been kept a secret from us for too long. And it's time for you to reclaim your authority and begin creating the world you genuinely want—complete with the people you want there.

So, if you take these actions, the person you have your eye on will be compelled to gravitate toward you.

The rule applies.

No More Manifesting of Hope

This is neither a gimmick nor an attempt to mislead you with promises of instant manifestations.

I prioritize long-lasting effects.

I can assure you that there won't be any more failed or incomplete appearances. I'm going to demonstrate to you how to accurately and successfully generate a meaningful relationship—possibly even marriage if that's what you desire—with the person you've always wanted.
But you must put in the effort.
Stay with me if that's what you're after. Because we're getting deep here, boys!

Before we even start the seven-step process of manifesting your ideal spouse, we'll go over all the preliminary work you need to complete. And make some pointed inquiries like...

Are you truly prepared to accept the invitation of your ideal partner?
If so, we'll continue to the following section where I'll walk you through the process of altering your mentality, getting rid of any limiting ideas that might be impeding your desire, setting your intention correctly, and becoming the ideal match for the love you want.

Last but not least, I'll explain how to invoke the power of creation, appropriately picture your intended

outcome for the best outcomes, and disregard your present reality until your desired relationship with your SP manifests right before your eyes.

I've also included instructions on how to get rid of any outside interference and how to spot indicators that your manifestation is approaching to make sure I've covered all your bases.

Over time, the process of achieving a goal won't take as much time.

Setting an intention, settling into a state of relaxation, and repeatedly

envisioning the desired outcome will suffice. and presto!

Just like in the movies, the love of your life will suddenly appear in front of you as you are mindlessly strolling down the street or entering a café, knocking you off your feet, and making you fall head over heels in love.

We have some work to do first, though, before you can truly live out your "happily ever after"!

Chapter 2

How to Manifest Love Using the Law of Attraction

The Law of Attraction: The Science Behind It According to research on quantum physics, the reality is created by the act of observation. When you concentrate on something, it comes to you and manifests in your reality.

The relationship between quantum mechanics and relating to the law of attraction. The study of the smallest energy particles is known as quantum physics.

When noticed (when we focus our attention on them), energy particles

behave differently, according to physicists.

According to the quantum entanglement theory, which holds that two particles behave as though they are one despite their physical separation from one another, everything in the cosmos is interconnected. This natural occurrence demonstrates how everything in the world is interconnected. Even if they are separated by large distances, one object cannot be affected without also having an impact on the other.

According to the Law of Attraction, our vibration and the things we focus on will attract each other.

Since everything is related and energy behaves differently when it is observed, your environment may be changed by the vibrational frequency of your thoughts, which are also energy. In other words, whatever you concentrate on or think about, is what manifests in your world.

So, what did you discover today here? that the Law of Attraction (the fundamental law of magnetism) is a powerful force that can radically alter your circumstances.

Let's now examine how it functions.

The Workings of the Law of Attraction

Everything in the cosmos is energy, according to the Law of Energy, one of the 12 universal principles. EVERYTHING.

Every living thing, including plants, animals, people, and objects, moves and vibrates at a specific frequency, down down to the smallest particle.

Even your emotions and thoughts are forms of energy.

You are also emitting a signal (or frequency) that attracts everything that matches it according to the Law of Attraction, which states simply that "like attracts like."

Whatever we put our energy, focus, and attention to—whether it's something nasty or something positive—we attract.

The cosmos is impartial. Only these laws are being followed in its operations.

Therefore, it is not punishing you. If your love life has been more tragic

and less happily-ever-after, and if life isn't going the way you'd intended, it's likely because you've been subconsciously attracting low vibrational situations into your life through negative ideas, limiting beliefs, and lower-level emotions.

Let's look more closely at how your vibrational frequency affects your manifestation now, as well as some strategies for increasing it.

Chapter 3

What is the frequency of your vibrations?

We can feel a variety of different emotions on any given day, let's face it. So, as a result of our ideas and feelings, our frequency is always changing.

You vibrate at a higher frequency when you're happy. Additionally, you vibrate at a lower frequency when you're unhappy. It seems very easy, doesn't it?

Yes and no, I suppose.

You can't just turn on a happy disposition and keep it all the time,

believing that your artificial grin will boost your vibration and draw your ideal life to you right away.

More complicated than that.

Because what we bring into our lives is determined by our dominant emotional vibration, which is where we are most of the time.

And that, my friends, is determined by the colossal amount of limiting ideas, memories, and emotional triggers (all your baggage) that you've unwittingly gathered throughout your existence.

Because to manifest something, you must energetically align with its frequency.

And you must emit the frequency of love if you want to attract love

(whether it be with a particular person or in general).

And it can be a significant step up from where you are currently.

However, you CAN NOT materialize a long-lasting, loving relationship with them until you align your frequency with that of your SP (get on their wavelength). You won't be prepared to resist them.

How do you raise your energy frequency to meet love?

To put it simply, you must have complete alignment between your mind, body, and emotions.

And when it comes to manifesting a specific person, many people leave out the important fact that no amount of LOA techniques can help you if you are not by your desire.

Let's be real here.

You only really want to be drawn to this particular person because you think that, in a relationship with them, you'll finally find true happiness.

However, to 'have' them, you must first be genuinely happy. Anything less than that won't work.
How do I align with my desire, you may be asking yourself right now?
Let me now describe how this works.

Chapter 4

How To Align With Your Desire

You're reading this article because you have your eye on a particular person with whom you'd like to materialize a relationship, regardless of how much of an energetic distance there is between you and your desire or how far it is.

And if you aren't already in a love connection with your SP, something is preventing you from becoming so.
Investigating that is the first step. (Oooh, it can also be a whole bunch of pessimistic ninnies keeping you back!)
After that, we'll need to clear away the overgrown jungle that has grown in your mind, pull all of the weeds, and establish a brand-new garden.
Prepare to dig in deep! While you're at it, grab a nice set of gardening gloves.
Because things are about to become quite messy inside...
yet I haven't even scratched the surface of the entire "garden" concept.

Okay, so you must alter your present attitudes, convictions, and routines if you wish to match your ambition.

WARNING! The actual work starts right here.

Get Your Mind Ready for Successful Manifestation

When purposefully manifesting your dream, you must first prepare the ground and eliminate all doubt from your thoughts to ensure success.

You must let go of any resistance you might be holding onto to manifest love with your particular partner.

Now is the moment to consider your readiness for love.

You must be sincere with yourself. Because your seeds of desire won't ever bloom if any unanswered

questions are lying below the surface. They'll prevent you from manifesting. It's that easy.

So let's get beyond these challenges before putting in the effort to attract our ideal partner.

By addressing these concerns first, you'll prevent wasted time and future disappointment from manifestations that don't happen or only happen partially.

The Following Questions to Ask Yourself

Do you think the Law of Attraction exists and can help you?

Do you genuinely think that you could be with this person?

Do you think you deserve to be loved?

Do you adore yourself and think that, with or without another person, you are whole and complete?

Are you prepared to put in the effort necessary to accomplish your goal?
Congratulations if your response to these questions was "yes." Up here, things are going to get amazing!
You are now prepared to begin drawing in your SP!
However, it's more likely that you declined to answer some of those. Thus, this is my advice.
Steps to Take

1. ESTABLISH FOR YOURSELF THAT THE LAW

OF ATTRACTION IS EFFECTIVE.

You will never experience success with the Law of Attraction if you don't believe in it. So, back it up.

Find examples of other people's success. Alternately, start attempting to manifest minor things like a good parking spot, a complimentary drink, or praise.

Anything that will demonstrate its veracity to you.

2. REMOVE YOUR SP FROM THE PEDESTAL

You won't be a vibrational match to that person if, deep down, you don't think it's feasible that you might ever

be with them, or if you've placed them on such a pedestal that you think they're beyond your reach. You're merely making your desire face more opposition. You're telling the universe that this individual is not someone you deserve.

This person you're obsessed with, your crush, is NOT so powerful that they won't give you their time or affection. They are merely regular individuals. Consider them to be one. No one wants to date their stalker, for this reason.

3. BOOST YOUR SENSE OF WORTH.

This leads me to my next point. How do you understand yourself precisely now?

Before we move on, it's important to concentrate on boosting your self-esteem and developing some real self-love if you feel undeserving of love or like you NEED your SP to complete you.

You cannot expect another individual to completely satisfy your needs or serve as the "cause" for your happiness.

To them, it's unfair.

You must approach creating this person from the perspective that YOU ARE ALREADY WHOLE AND COMPLETE.

Hence, from a perspective of WANTING them rather than NEEDING them.

Nobody must keep you content. You have to do it.

And no one wants to date a needy or clingy person.

You will only attract individuals who value and respect you if you work on developing a good sense of self-worth. And when you discover true self-love,

that's when the windows of true love start to open.

Chapter 5

The 7 Steps to Finding Love with a Particular Person

1. Tell the universe you want to be with that particular person.

You might be saying, "Well, hell! The world ought to already be aware of my desires.

However, I can guarantee that it doesn't. Because if you aren't already with your SP, you are undoubtedly sending conflicting messages to the cosmos.

Your desire to date, be in a serious relationship with or marry your chosen partner must be evident in all of your thoughts, feelings, and actions.

Establishing a specific intention... and putting it in writing, is the best way to do that.

Steps to Take

PLACE YOUR SP ORDER WITH CRYSTAL CLEAR INTENTION.

This is the exciting part, yay! Now is the moment to pull out your journal and start daydreaming about your ideal partner.

Describe in detail how you want to be treated by them, a normal day with them, the topics you'd discuss, and the locations you'd go.

Will you two be one of those married couples who spend every moment together, or will you both be more independent and take regular breaks to do your own thing?

What characteristics of their personalities do you admire? What about you do people adore? What about them draws you in?

Define the connection. Be precise without being absurdly rigid. Not a Ken doll, but a real person.

And the greatest approach to working out all the specifics, becoming crystal clear on exactly what you want to materialize, and imprinting your wish on your subconscious mind is to put everything on paper.

Because it will obstruct you every step of the way if the subconscious isn't on board with what you want to produce.

DON'T LOSE SIGHT OF WHAT YOU WANT.

What you concentrate on, you receive. You will draw more of the same if you constantly think about what you DON'T WANT rather than what YOU DO WANT.

The negative remarks are not separated from the good ones by the

Law of Attraction. You only get what you pay attention to, not anything else.

Negative statements must be avoided because of this. As a result, refrain from using phrases like "They NEVER lose their temper," "They NEVER leave the toilet seat up," etc.

Change it to a positive phrase, such as "They ALWAYS put the toilet seat down," "They are ALWAYS in control of their emotions," etc.

You see what I mean. We're teaching ourselves to speak positively and to see the good in everything.

Be mindful of the ideas and feelings you focus on and hold onto. Because you must only concentrate on the things you DO WANT if you want to apply the Law of Attraction to manifest love with a particular individual.

Another justification for writing out your intended aim is that. It's a terrific method to direct your attention away from the things you don't want.

2. Disprove Strict Beliefs

What are the underlying presumptions or erroneous ideas you

possess that are preventing you from manifesting?

Steps to Take

WRITE DOWN YOUR LIMITING BELIEFS IN A LIST

What ideas do you hold about relationships, love, and other topics? Do you think that all men are athletes?

Does every woman desert you? Do all relationships fail?

Make a list of all your limiting beliefs by picking up a pen and paper.

BE AWARE OF YOUR THOUGHTS

Observe your thoughts as they arise during the day as they relate to your person, relationships, love, etc.

What sets you off? What causes you to react?

Do you ever notice that a certain thought comes to mind whenever you witness a couple kissing, arguing, having a conversation, etc.?

What happens when you watch a movie?

Note any persistent thoughts you have and capture them in writing. (Do you see a pattern here? Take notes on everything! This makes new beliefs more subconsciously ingrained and will help you monitor your progress.)

EDIT YOUR LIMITING PERSPECTIVES

Now add all the unfavorable ideas you had today to your list of limiting beliefs. Then, turn them around and rework them such that they are empowering affirmations.

You should include these as affirmations in your morning ritual, which I'll cover in step #3.

To help retrain your subconscious mind, you could even want to record these comments and listen to them throughout the day.

3. Modify Your Mentality

It's time to adjust your vibrational set point and form new habits. Affirmations, scripting, and gratitude journals are probably not unfamiliar to you unless you're new to manifestation.

These can be effective tools to help you stay on the correct path and

realign yourself daily with your desires.

Create a Daily Manifestation Schedule

Establishing a morning manifestation ritual with affirmations, scripts, and gratitude will help you get the best start to the day.

To attract more of the things you want into your life, such as the love relationship you desire with a specific person, it is the ideal method to boost your strength and personality first thing in the morning.

Additionally, by ending your day with more positive affirmations, expressions of gratitude, and visualizations of what you want, you're implanting high-vibe feelings as well as the seeds of your desire into your subconscious mind, which it will continue to digest while you're sleeping deeply.

The first thing you do when you wake up in the morning and just before you go to sleep is "wonderful gateway moments" in the day.

Your brain shifts into the Theta state at this point.

You have control over your subconscious mind when you're in the theta stage. This makes it the ideal time to practice affirmations, scripts, visualizations, or sowing any change-related seeds.

Steps to Take

MANIFESTATION ROUTINE FOR ATTRACTING YOUR SP IN THE MORNING

Here is what you will do as soon as your alarm goes off in the morning:

- **Start each day with gratitude.**

Take out your journal and list five things for which you are thankful in the present. If you need assistance with this step or find it challenging to list five things each day for which you are grateful.

- **Write in a Dream Life Journal**

Writing about your ideal existence will generate a lot of momentum and change your perspective to reflect your desires.

Therefore, devote 5–10 minutes a day to writing in your notebook about the relationship you envision for yourself. Imagine yourself in the future, enjoying the most wonderful and delicious relationship possible with your sweetheart.

Use the present tense while writing and "I am" statements rather than "I will" statements. Therefore, imagine that your desire has already been fulfilled.

materialized. Live that fantasy and experience what it's like to be happy with that particular individual.

And always close your entries in your journal with thankfulness.

I'm extremely grateful to the universe!

- **Create a list of your daily affirmations.**

Decide which aspects of your life or personality you want to improve on. It's time to adopt the personality of the person you hope to date.

You'll also draw the person you've always wanted to be with since "like attracts like."

You'll apply the affirmations you wrote when you wrote down your limiting beliefs in step #2 here. For instance, "I deserve love," "All the people I am drawn to are drawn to me," or "I only draw stable, happy, loving individuals who appreciate me."

Every morning, jot down your affirmations and repeat them aloud for a few minutes. Make it a habit of saying these encouraging things throughout the day as well, though, to fully rewire them into your subconscious. If you want a reminder, you can set a timer on your phone.

Recall the affirmation recording we mentioned in the part above about "Limiting Beliefs"? If not, allow me to remind you briefly. Make a recording of yourself speaking your affirmations aloud in a soothing tone. Add some calming, uplifting music as well.

Now take out that bad boy and listen to it all day long. The optimum time to reprogram the subconscious mind is at night while you're asleep.

- **Create a daily manifesto list.**

Each day, list 3-5 goals you'd like to achieve.

Choose little manifestations that you won't encounter much resistance to,

such as getting a free coffee or a compliment.

The outcomes will be recorded after each day.

This not only strengthens your belief in the power of the Law of Attraction but also trains your manifestation muscles. Keeping note of your everyday manifestations will help you become more adept at achieving your larger wishes if you're new to manifesting.

My friend, perfect practice makes perfect.

You'll also start to realize that your little wants materialize far more quickly and easily than your larger ones. That's because you don't care about the outcome and are less

resistant to them. You frequently completely disregard them.

Your huge aspirations will manifest much more quickly if you can accomplish that with them.

ROUTINE OF THE EVENING MANIFESTATION

- **Review Your Day First**

Before going to sleep every night, consider your day.

You might even want to take a moment to rewrite the things that went wrong in your handy dandy notebook. This aids in solidifying your desire to alter those things in your thinking. If not, you'd simply forget about them.

Additionally, it gives you something to review in the future to evaluate whether you've made any progress.

- **Keep a daily manifesto results log.**

Reread the list of manifestations you made the previous morning. Have any of them appeared today? It appeared you've recorded throughout the past few days.

Maybe something that was on your list from yesterday came true today.

Make a note of what happened to you that day. How long it took, whether there were any telltale signals, synchronicities, your responses,

feelings, and thoughts, as well as how they manifested.
This will provide you with a point of comparison so you can show yourself that this is real and effective.

- **Thank you**

All the good things that happened to you during the day should be recorded in your journal. Spend some time feeling proud of yourself and thankful for those accomplishments.
By doing this, you're not only raising your vibration but also teaching your subconscious mind to bring more positive things into your life.

- **Visualize the Goal**

You want to see the brief scene you produced of you being in a loving relationship with your special someone in the moments just before you fall asleep. You should provide as much information and feelings as you can. Set the scene using all five senses, then play it over and over until you nod off.

By far, the most crucial stage of the creative process is visualization. And there are many factors to consider to manifest correctly and successfully.

Continue reading to learn exactly what you must do. I'll walk you through the procedure in step #5.

4...Adapt Yourself To the Person You Want to Attract

You must strive to be a happy, loving, confident person if you want to attract someone who shares those traits.

Recall the earlier list you made of qualities you hope to see in a certain person. If you want to draw that person into your life, you must nurture those qualities.

Not that you have to be their twin, mind you. That would be unsettling. Nobody wants to date someone who is a carbon copy of themselves.

However, if you want to be a match for your SP, you do need to possess similar traits.

- **PURPOSE YOURSELF**

Turn your attention away from that particular individual and toward yourself. Give your wellbeing first importance.

Make an effort to be cheerful. things that energize you for the day. Take that pal to lunch.

I last saw you a year ago. Take a run. Bathe in bubbles. Or pick up that novel you've been implying to read.

One of the best ways to improve your vibration is to take care of your physical and mental health. Show yourself, then

- **DO SOME HEART CHAKRA WORK**

Your heart chakra is a real pump that releases the energy of love into the universe when it is opened and expanded.

Spend a few seconds thinking about the things you enjoy about our planet. family, close friends, your kids, or animals.

Feel the emotion of love in your body. All the warm fuzzies you experience when you are around or think about the things you love, including the warmth, the way your heart flutters, and the smile that spreads across your face.

You'll start to glow.

Now try your best to cling to that sensation. Float in it.

Because you must resonate with the frequency of love if you want to attract love. As a result, practice tuning into the proper frequency every day.

You can also use mantras, gratitude, crystals, affirmations, and meditation to open your heart chakra.

- FORGIVENESS

Make an effort to forgive. You can prevent the manifestation of a love relationship with that particular individual by holding onto your resentment, old hurts, or memories from the past.

Do you need to make amends to them for anything?
Release whatever hatred or resentment you may be holding inside, regardless of who the person is (your ex, someone who has put you in the "friend-zone," a stranger, or whatever your specific circumstance may be).
Even if it means forgiving them for not already having declared their love for you.
Go deep. You might even discover that you need to extend forgiveness to persons you've dated in the past or to someone who may have wronged you in the past.

Both yourself and them should be forgiven. Because low vibrational emotions like resentment, guilt, humiliation, and rage are dragging you down.

5. See Your Imagined Act in Motion

The visualization method developed by Neville Goddard is by far the most effective for achieving any goal. And using your imagination's power to create a romantic relationship with a certain person is the best approach to make it happen.

- CREATE YOUR IMAGINARY SCENE

Start by creating your imaginal act, which is a succinct, elaborate scene of what you wish. When trying to fill in all the details, writing them down can be helpful.

Make sure to describe in great detail each of the five senses.

Put yourself in the situation.

How are you doing? Anyone there? What do they have on? What noises are you hearing? How do you feel?

Before you begin envisioning it, be sure to write down every single detail.

- **LET GO AND ENTER A MEDITATIVE STATE**

Next, either through meditation or while lying in bed just before going to sleep, induce a state of meditation.

How do you tell if you're in the right state for meditation?

You'll transition into the Theta brainwave state, which is a highly relaxed level of consciousness.

You become completely unaware of all concerns, future projections, physical attachments, and the outer world. You'll have a profound sense of inner calm and emotional stability.

- VISUALIZE IN FIRST PERSON AT ALL TIMES

Then start picturing your mental film, making careful to picture the scene from the first person's perspective. Your desired scene might come true for someone else if you picture it from a third-person

perspective as if you were watching a movie.

Participate in your imaginary act since you are its major character.

- **PRO MANIFESTATION TIP**

If your scene involves you being married to your specific person, play with your wedding ring while you're imagining it. You can also look down to see your hands or the hands of your specific person wrapped around yours. This serves to immerse you in the viewpoint of the protagonist and serves as a reminder to stick with the first person.

- **REPEAT**

Play the scene repeatedly until it feels natural.
Restart at the beginning when you get to the conclusion. until you nod off, and keep acting out the scene.
Do this every night until you begin to believe that the fictitious incident has already taken place. It can take many days, or even weeks or months.

- **EMOTION IS CRUCIAL.**

The secret is to visualize your scene while conjuring up the overpowering feeling of happiness (in a natural way).

When you visualize, you should feel as though you are actually in the imagined scene. Now it's occurring.

You are currently blissed out and have everything you wanted!

Would you, therefore, feel "blah" about being with your particular individual at last? Not at all, not at all!

You would experience a deep sense of delight and profound thankfulness. Draw on previous times when you have felt that way and invoke those feelings as you picture your imagined setting. Feel the surroundings.

It's not an artificial or forced emotion. Even though at first, it could seem that way. But continue to train. Continue imagining the happiness until it seems genuine.

Amplify it now.

You'll know you've planted the seed when you experience that overpowering sensation of extreme joy followed by a wave of relaxation and contentment.

6. Trust the Universe; Let it Go

It's time to take a step back and give the universe your wish. mostly because it is competent. It also wants you to know that it has you, sweetheart!

So step aside and let the cosmos take care of itself.

Stop attempting to force events to occur according to your schedule.

Avoid pursuing your SP. Because you repel what you pursue.

We're talking about vibrations, after all. Your particular person will sense desperation if it comes out in your energy.

And they will rush away from you as quickly as their tiny feet will carry them.

Because the love you want to experience is not what desperation is a homing beacon for, but rather greater desperation.

Not that you should refrain from taking "inspired action," though (which does not come from a place of fear or control).

It's the universe gently nudging you in the right direction, leaving a trail of breadcrumbs leading to your goal.

So, only take action if you are motivated or prompted to do so by your intuition.
And do it from a place of enthusiasm and assurance rather than desperation or scarcity.

- **AVOID CONTINUING TO DRAW UP THE SEED**

Stop checking on your seed of desire once you've successfully planted it. Or it won't ever expand.
In other words, stop worrying about when it will happen, how it will happen, or what "the middle" will look like.
Stop envisioning a text from your SP or bumping into them over the weekend to create a date if your final

goal is to be in love, committed relationship with (or even married to) them.

Only yourself are you sabotaging. Because if you begin to interfere with the middle, you can wind up causing a whole host of challenges and setbacks that could completely derail your manifestation.

Therefore, after you've sown the seed, let it grow.

- **DON'T BE OBSESSED WITH IT**

When you are constantly fixated on something.

You're not allowing your passion to expand or breathe when you think about it.

You're also telling the universe you don't have it when you NEED something or become overly connected to the result. The cosmos will therefore have to continue withholding it from you.

It only matches your vibration. the sound of lack.

You must have the impression that you ARE already with the person you wish to be with. You must focus on experiencing abundance and love. As much as you can, cultivate that emotion and dwell there.

Because everything in this universe that you desire will be drawn to you when you radiate love, just like a moth is drawn to a flame.

It is the quickest approach to attracting the partner of your dreams.

- **BE PATIENT, EVERYONE IS PUSHING YOU OUT.**

The idea that "everyone is you pushed out" is related to Neville Goddard's teachings. On one level, it alludes to the idea that every individual in your world is a reflection of your interior state. And everyone is playing the part that you have given them in your head.

On a much deeper level, however, this idea reveals the unspoken reality that every living thing on the planet is bound together by the same awareness.

The same knowledge that permeates through you and everyone else also permeates through me.

With this in mind, be aware that once you successfully plant your desire into the field of awareness that unites every person on the planet, it starts making all kinds of arrangements to place the appropriate individuals in the appropriate situations at the appropriate times to advance your manifestation.

Therefore, depending on who you're trying to manifest, the time it takes for your SP to manifest in your reality will vary.

It can take some time for the universe to make all the required arrangements to get you two together if your particular individual is

already in a relationship, live halfway over the world, or involves any other complicated situations.

You'll need to exercise patience while waiting. Keep your energy high, cling to the emotion of love, and act as if your wish has already come true.

7…Live at the End

Living, in the end, is a condition of being, not a technique.

This is the main cause of many manifestations failing. Most individuals trip themselves up at this step since it is by far the hardest.

Neville's idea of "Living in the End" tells us to visualize any state and stay there.

If you want to attract a specific person into your life, you must fervently imagine yourself already having the most wonderful connection possible with that person. Or, live fully as though your wish has already been fulfilled.

Steps to Take

- **HOW TO BEHAVE AS IF YOUR DESIRE HAS BEEN FULFILLED**

What would it be like to be with the person you want to be with?

Imagine what your life would be like after you've drawn your ideal partner.

Avoid considering your wish. Living off of it

To put it another way, you have to take on the form of your future self and act as if your wish has already materialized. Every day, you should think and behave as the person you want to be—the one who is already with your particular person.

Would you be checking their social media if you were currently married to your SP or in a committed relationship with them? Would you be expressing your loneliness to your friends? Would you be aching for them so badly?

Oh, no way!

You'd be sincerely joyful, giving thanks to the stars that your true fairy tale came true, and concentrating on realizing other goals.

You wouldn't need to concentrate on attracting a particular individual because they are already in your life. In other terms, you'd have fulfillment and satisfaction. After Thanksgiving dinner, you feel satisfied and no longer have a hankering for food.

So be satisfied.

- **IGNORE YOUR PRESENT SITUATION**

Everything that is manifesting in your present reality is a reflection of your previous energy. In other words, everything that is happening in your life right now is a product of all of your previous feelings, thoughts, and beliefs.

It could take some time for your current circumstances to change when you change your frequency.

Similar to what happens when a guitarist plays a guitar string in a vast auditorium, there is an echo effect. The sound of the note played takes some time to travel through the walls and return to the audience's ears. Therefore, even after the musician has gone on and

picked the next chord, the hand of that note can still be heard.

- **DO NOT IMPACT PARTIAL MANIFESTATIONS POSITIVELY**

Fight the desire to lose faith or throw a fit if things don't turn out exactly the way you expected them to or even if the contrary of what you wanted occurs in your reality.

Because a bad response might undermine your efforts and delay manifestation.

You can't perceive the vast picture from your finite human perspective. You are

not privy to all that goes on behind the scenes.

Therefore, what appears to you to be confusion or unfavorable occurrences may be the most ideal means for the universe to grant your want.

Chapter 6

How to Get Rid of a Third Party

You can still attract the precise person you want into your life even if they are already involved with someone else, are married or are simply hung up on someone else.

It's quite easy.

Avoid concentrating on the outsider

We build our reality if you've been paying attention. By focusing on what we want to attract, we achieve that.

Therefore, all you need to do to get rid of a third party is to not think about them.

Don't get crazy if you see your SP with someone else.

Because you're putting up a barrier to your desire when you stress over your particular individual being with someone else.

And each time you respond negatively to this outsider, you make them a part of your reality. What you DON'T WANT is becoming more pronounced.

Just concentrate on the conclusion. You with your particular companion.

The only way to completely exclude the third party from the situation is to do that.

Never pay them any attention at all. You don't intend to hurt them in any way. only that in YOUR world they don't exist.

Keep Outsiders Out of Your Imaginary Act.

And they should under no circumstances appear in your imagined deed!

You should only be imagining once your wish has been fulfilled, anyway. Therefore, they have no business being present at all. You haven't even had a thought.

You know you're already with your special individual if you're living from the end. And why would your SP be offended or even consider this third person if he or she is already

madly in love with you and only has eyes for you?

Even so, they shouldn't be a problem.

Now, this does not mean that you should ignore this third party individual if you run into them or come into contact with them physically in your present reality. That will simply create more obstacles in the way of your manifestation.

Be a normal person. But don't dwell on them, pay them unfavorable attention, or let them inside your head, which is ultimately where you're living.

It's that easy.

Okay, I can tell you're eager to get started.

After completing all of the necessary tasks (dotting all of your i's and crossing all of your t's), you may be wondering whether there will be any telltale signs that your manifestation is approaching.

You can count on there being indicators, I can guarantee you that. So let's interview a limited number.

Chapter 7

5 Indicators That Your Manifestation Is Coming

Once the seed is planted, you can start to notice indications that the universe is carrying out your will and your manifestation is getting close. Playing the waiting game with your desire and looking for indications is not something I suggest. However, if you do start to perceive indications from the universe, it might reassure you and strengthen your conviction that everything you're experiencing is true.

As a result, pay attention and note any signs you encounter in your journal.

You can then use it as a reference point whenever you need to be reminded that you are about to begin a meaningful relationship with someone in particular.

However, resist the want to constantly check for indications that aren't there and urgently look for consolation. You'll just succeed in depressing your vibration and delaying your yearning.

Here are some potential sights:

- An angel or a series of numbers

This is a signal that your vibration has increased and that circumstances are working in your favor. These figures provide comfort that you are moving in the correct direction or that a shift is imminent.

- **Coincidences start to happen**

What exactly are coincidences? These are events that, despite our perceptions that they are coincidences, are linked in a way that neither science nor reason can explain. For you and your SP to be together, these things happen because the universe is using its magic to put the right people in the right places at the right times.

- **An Overflowing Love is Appearing in Your Reality**

You start to realize that love surrounds you everywhere! People are overheard discussing it. You may see couples making out all over the place. More than normal, people are connecting online and raving about their partners. You notice more examples of love in your reality because you are vibrating at the frequency of love, which is an indication that you are. Recognize it as a sign that your special someone is approaching and appreciate it!

- **You feel as though your desire has already been fulfilled**

A calmness overtakes you when your desires and actions are perfectly

aligned. You have let go of every opposition, and you are certain that your goal is coming true.

- **Difficulties and Barriers**

These are a little challenging. But don't be negative in your response to these

challenges. Keep in mind that what we perceive as a challenge may be the universe's preferred method of realizing our desires. Alternatively, the universe may be putting obstacles in your way because you need to

learn certain lessons before moving forward with your manifestation.

Chapter 8

Conclusion

Everything occurs at the perfect time. Your goal will undoubtedly come true when everything is in perfect alignment. But as every wish is unique, the length of time it takes to come true will depend on your circumstances.

So, I'm afraid I can't provide you with a certain time frame. Nobody can.

The loving relationship you've been wishing for with your particular person WILL manifest if you've completed the steps in this guide and are keeping a vibratory set point of love.

And once you've given your passion a chance to grow, don't sit around and wait for it to bloom. Pass on. All systems go!

Sow one more seed. then another Continue sowing seeds and bringing more incredible things into your reality.

And before you know it, you'll be so preoccupied building your universe that you'll be taken by surprise when...S-M-A-C-K! You charge head-on towards your life's love. and,

if your imagination was correct, they'll have a happy ending.

www.ingramcontent.com/pod-product-compliance
Lightning Source LLC
LaVergne TN
LVHW050328160826
845677LV00014B/3563

9798846639928